I'M ALLERGIC TO TREE NUTS

By Walter LaPlante

Gareth Stevens
PUBLISHING

Please visit our website, www.garethstevens.com. For a free color catalog of all our high-quality books, call toll free 1-800-542-2595 or fax 1-877-542-2596.

Library of Congress Cataloging-in-Publication Data

Names: LaPlante, Walter, author.
Title: I'm allergic to tree nuts / Walter LaPlante.
Description: New York : Gareth Stevens Publishing, [2019] | Series: I'm allergic | Includes bibliographical references and index.
Identifiers: LCCN 2018023553| ISBN 9781538229088 (library bound) | ISBN 9781538232460 (pbk.) | ISBN 9781538232477 (6 pack)
Subjects: LCSH: Food allergy–Juvenile literature. | Nuts–Juvenile literature.
Classification: LCC RC596 .L382 2019 | DDC 616.97/5–dc23
LC record available at https://lccn.loc.gov/2018023553

Published in 2019 by
Gareth Stevens Publishing
111 East 14th Street, Suite 349
New York, NY 10003

Designer: Laura Bowen
Editor: Kate Mikoley

Photo credits: cover, p. 1 (main) Photographee.eu/Shutterstock.com; cover, p. 1 (bowl) exopixel/Shutterstock.com; p. 5 Jupiterimages/Photolibrary/Getty Images; p. 7 (brazil nuts) zcw/Shutterstock.com; p. 7 (walnuts, hazelnuts) Tim UR/Shutterstock.com; p. 7 (cashews) Hong Vo/Shutterstock.com; p. 7 (whole almonds) Loadmaster/Wikimedia Commons; p. 7 (shelled almonds) MARKELLOS/Wikimedia Commons; p. 7 (pistachios) Grendelkhan/Wikimedia Commons; p. 9 Elizaveta Galitckaia/Shutterstock.com; p. 11 KidStock/Blend Images/Getty Images; p. 13 AFP/Stringer/Getty Images; p. 15 Andrey_Popov/Shutterstock.com; p. 17 Olena Yakobchuk/Shutterstock.com; p. 19 Visage/Stockbyte/Getty Images; p. 21 Streetfly Studio/JR Carvey/Blend Images/Getty Images.

Printed in the United States of America

CPSIA compliance information: Batch #CW19GS: For further information contact Gareth Stevens, New York, New York at 1-800-542-2595.

CONTENTS

Oh, Nuts! .4

Nuts That Aren't 8

What Happens. 10

Check It Out! 14

No More Nuts 16

Glossary. 22

For More Information. 23

Index 24

Boldface words appear in the glossary.

Oh, Nuts!

Have you ever felt sick after eating some trail mix? Or a nutty candy bar? You might have an **allergy** to tree nuts! This is one of the most common food allergies in the United States.

Tree nuts grow on trees! They have a hard shell. Tree nuts include many nuts people like to eat. Almonds, cashews, hazelnuts, pecans, pine nuts, walnuts, pistachios, Brazil nuts, and macadamia nuts are all tree nuts.

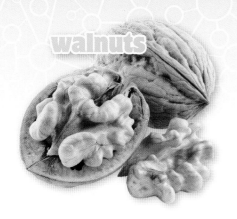

walnuts

pistachios

almonds

hazelnuts

Brazil nuts

cashews

Nuts That Aren't

Peanuts aren't tree nuts. They're **legumes**. But, many people who are allergic to peanuts are also allergic to tree nuts. Coconuts aren't nuts at all! They're fruit seeds. Most people with tree nut allergies can eat coconut safely.

What Happens

Someone with a tree nut allergy may have a tummy ache or feel like throwing up after eating tree nuts. They may have trouble swallowing or feel **itchy** in their throat or mouth. They may get a runny nose, too.

One **serious** allergic **reaction** is called anaphylaxis (an-uh-fuh-LAK-sis). It causes breathing trouble. People with allergies may carry a special shot they can use if this happens. In the United States, tree nut allergies are one of the most common causes of anaphylaxis.

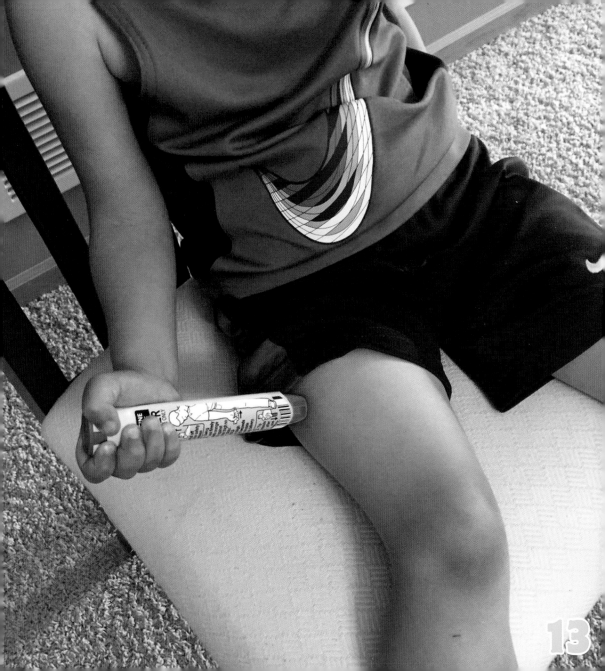

Check It Out!

Doctors may do a blood test to be sure a person's allergy is to tree nuts. They may also **prick** the skin and put some kinds of tree nut on it. If the area becomes red and raised, that means there's an allergy!

No More Nuts

Medicines can help someone with tree nut allergies feel better. However, to stop allergic reactions, you need to stay away from tree nuts! Many foods with tree nuts in them have labels that say so. Still, it's important to read the **ingredients** of a food before eating it.

Sometimes, a food's ingredients could have touched tree nuts. People who have tree nut allergies need to stay away from these foods, too. Baked goods such as cookies and cakes may cause problems for those with tree nut allergies for this reason.

About 10 percent of children with a tree nut allergy will outgrow it! However, if you aren't one of these people, it's easier than ever to live happily with a tree nut allergy. Just be sure to check your food labels!

21

GLOSSARY

allergy: a sensitivity to usually harmless things in the surroundings called allergens, such as foods, pollen, or insect stings

ingredient: one of the things used to make food

itchy: having an unpleasant feeling on your skin or inside your mouth or nose that makes you want to scratch

legume: a type of plant (such as beans or peas) with seeds that grow in long pods

medicine: a drug taken to make a sick person well

prick: to make a very small hole in something

reaction: the way your body acts because of certain matter or surroundings

serious: having a dangerous outcome

FOR MORE INFORMATION

BOOKS

Jorgensen, Katrina. *No Peanuts, No Problem!: Easy and Delicious Nut-Free Recipes for Kids with Allergies.* North Mankato, MN: Capstone Press, 2017.

Potts, Francesca. *All About Allergies.* Minneapolis, MN: Super Sandcastle, 2018.

WEBSITES

Learning About Allergies
kidshealth.org/en/kids/allergies.html
Visit this website to learn more about all kinds of allergies.

Tree Nut Allergy
www.kidswithfoodallergies.org/page/tree-nut-allergy.aspx
Find a list of what to look for on food labels to help you stay away from tree nuts.

INDEX

almonds 6, 7

anaphylaxis 12

blood test 14

Brazil nuts 6, 7

cashews 6,7

coconuts 8

doctor 14

food labels 16, 20

hazelnuts 6, 7

ingredients 16, 18

legumes 8

macadamia nuts 6

medicine 16

outgrowing allergies 20

peanuts 8

pecans 6

pine nuts 6

pistachios 6, 7

shells 6

skin test 14

symptoms 10

United States 4, 12

walnuts 6, 7